BUREAUCRATIC SPEED BUMPS AND ECOLOGICAL TREAD MARKS:

Environmental Policy Making in the Ontario Government, 1988-1993

Presentation by

David McRobert[1]

February 14, 1994

Presented to
Faculty of Environmental Studies
York University

North York, Ont.

(Revised slightly December 1995)

---

1   At the time of the presentation in February 1994, the author was Senior Policy and Research Analyst, Workplace Health and Safety Agency, 121 Bloor St. East, Suite 900, Toronto, ON. The new Ontario government announced the closure of the Agency in August 1995.

INTRODUCTION

In this paper I want to share with you some insights I gained about environmental policy-making while working in the Ontario government between 1988 and late last year when I left the Ontario Round Table on Environment and Economy for my current job.

I want to begin by explaining the two somewhat unusual phrases that I have used in the title of my talk.

I have borrowed the idea of "bureaucratic speed bumps" from Marcel Henrie, a federal senior civil servant. In his entertaining book, *The Mandarin Syndrome*, Henrie observes that senior bureaucrats are the speed bumps of their organizations. In other words, these civil servants ensure that ambitious young policy-makers don't start speeding through the policy development and approval process with new ideas and options intended to quickly alter the status quo. To my mind, this is a good metaphor for what senior bureaucrats do, and better, in some ways than the traditional metaphor of gatekeepers.

The phrase "ecological tread marks" was partly inspired by Professor Bill Rees at the Centre for Human Settlements at the University of British Columbia who, together with his colleagues, is currently engaged in important research on what he calls the ecological footprints of human activities.[1] In developing this phrase, I have tried to capture the essence of the ecological and social havoc that is wrought when public policy-making processes go slightly off track or are short-circuited by some combination of events. As a result, well-intentioned but sometimes poorly developed policies are implemented that have serious short-term or long-term environmental and social impacts.

I will be commenting on environmental policy making from a number of different perspectives. First, I have become a bit of a policy wonk[2], to use the language popularized by the Clinton Administration. Unfortunately, I still have not internalized all of the values that are required to be a superior policy wonk. During the two-year period I worked at the Waste Reduction Office[3] in the Ministry of the Environment and Energy (MOEE) I was one of a group of new policy people who tried to do front-tire bicycle wheelies off the speed bumps. Not only did we end up crashing into each other quite a few times, we also failed to promote our agenda in a coherent and effective way.

Secondly, my comments also reflect my six years of experience working off and on as a volunteer and a full-time waste management and global warming campaigner at Pollution Probe.

Finally, I will be commenting as a former student at FES who continues to struggle with the challenges of the deep ecological analysis.

---

1   With financial assistance from the Suzuki Foundation, Rees is trying to develop a new framework for analysing the ecological drain that first world residents place on global ecosystems. See: Mathis Wackernagel and William Rees, *Our Ecological Footprint: Reducing Human Impact on the Earth* (1995). Gabriola Island, BC: New Society Publishers.

2   Wonk, a term that is rumoured to have originated at Harvard University in the US, supposedly stands for "know" spelled backwards.

3   The Waste Reduction Office was established by the NDP government in early 1991. The WRO became the Waste Reduction Branch of the Conservation and Prevention Division in November 1993.

HOW THE POLICY MAKING PROCESS IS SUPPOSED TO WORK

To contextualize my comments, I want to briefly discuss how the policy process works in Ontario. As numerous commentators have pointed out, public policy is best defined as a set of inter-related and sometimes integrated decisions or non-decisions taken by political actors concerning the selection of goals and the means of achieving them.[4]

Invariably public policy is characterized by the need to deal with uncertainty and is intended to change or sustain human behaviour in certain ways. Those of us who seek to alter public policy tend to do so because we have an interventionist bent and feel we can make the world a better place. When I was a student at FES, many professors used to tell me to be careful because, to quote the old adage, "the road to hell is paved with good intentions". In retrospect, I realize now that there is more truth in this old adage than I was willing to admit as a student. But more on this in a few minutes.

Contrary to the theories offered by faculty here at York, my experience was that the policy development process is part science, part magic, and

---

4   For an entertaining and sometimes brilliant discussion of the policy process, see Giandomenico Majone, *Evidence, Argument and Persuasion in the Policy Process* (1989). New Haven: Cambridge University Press.

part luck but mainly sales and marketing. Unfortunately for me, when I first arrived at FES I worked with Steve Kline and Bill Leiss on their massive critique of Canadian advertising and I have a strong aversion to most sales and marketing techniques.[5] So I had to quickly learn to package my ideas for the government marketplace.

The lifeblood of policy development is the creation and critique of policy options. Usually a policy option starts out as a general idea about a problem or an issue that can come from the Minister, Cabinet, backbench MPPs, policy analysts, managers and even academics. If the idea has merit, usually it motivates further research and analysis to identify related issues.

As you can well imagine, policy ideas are circulating continually among staff within the government but most senior bureaucrats have their favourite ideas and theories. Moreover, knowledge is not necessarily power in the bureaucracy, power is power.[6] And one thing that makes senior and middle-level bureaucrats powerful is their actual control of how policy ideas are developed, marketed within the bureaucracy and then sold to key decision makers.

Generally discussion papers are drafted outlining proposals and options and these go back and forth in an iterative fashion between policy developers, senior managers and other staff for weeks or months on end. In most cases someone decides to bite the bullet and push the matter up to the decision makers.

---

5   My work assisted the researchers in the publication of their book with Sut Jhally: W. Leiss, Steve Kline and Sut Jhally, *Social Communication in Advertising* (1985). Toronto: Metheun.

6   This is a paraphrase of Bob Sass, one of the architects of modern occupational health and safety law and policy in Canada who has said, "knowledge is not power, power is power".

The key policy making instrument in Ontario is the cabinet submission.[7] These documents allow the minister and her or his political staff to crystallize the issues and options they want to present to various Cabinet Committees and then to Cabinet for final approval. At the Attorney General I reviewed more than a dozen cabinet submissions on a wide range of environmental, energy and aboriginal rights issues and at the WRO I co-authored three submissions and a number of internal MOEE policy documents.

The luck and magic come in to the cabinet submission process in its final stages. If you have magical powers you can ensure that all the documents that need to be signed by various staff, deputy ministers, and ministers are signed on time. (This is very unlikely to happen.) And if you are lucky, staff in Cabinet Office or the Premier's Office won't read the submissions to closely and start making or requesting last minute changes to the policy options that usually worsen the submissions rather than improve them.

Sometimes policy options are severely constrained or eliminated early in the process. For example, the current Ontario government decided to take both export of garbage out of the Greater Toronto Area (GTA) and solid waste incineration off the table in early 1991 and instead force York region to take Metro Toronto's garbage. Unfortunately there was little policy development work done by the bureaucracy in advance of these decisions and this meant the government was ill-prepared for the attacks launched on these decisions by their critics.

Once the submissions get through cabinet and the recommendations are "minuted", then the bureaucrats try to interpret them. Sometimes

---

7   For a full discussion of how the cabinet submission was to be prepared under the NDP administration, see Government of Ontario, Cabinet Office, *Cabinet Submission Guidelines* (1994). Toronto: Queen's Printer, May 1994. Available from the Ontario Government Bookstore for $5. It is likely that a new version of this guide will be prepared by the new Ontario government.

this leads to fights over the proper interpretation of the content and implications of a particular Cabinet minute.[8]

The ability of outsiders to influence this policy development process ranges widely. I found that consultants and lawyers with some government experience were by far the most effective lobbyists on behalf of their clients because they understood the system and usually had good contacts. In contrast, most environmentalists don't understand how governments work.[9] Their timing was often lousy because they didn't get the hot tips on the status of initiatives that bureaucrats provide to consultants who are willing to "smooze" with them over lunch.

One of the fascinating responses to this situation was that senior policy advisors in the Minister's office for the MOEE tried to overcome this disadvantage by regularly feeding crucial information and documents to environmental non-government organizations (ENGOs) so that the groups could improve their timing and their analysis. I found the Liberals did a quite a bit of this but the New Democratic Party (NDP) advisors tried to even the playing field more and took this practice to a new level.

Similarly, I found environmentalists did not understand that to be effective you have to put pressure on politicians and their staff but you also have to educate the bureaucracy about why they should do something and help them to sell your option in their discussion papers, briefing notes and cabinet submissions.

---

8   For example, the Cabinet Minute may specify that new legislation, regulations, and/or guidelines are to be developed but it may not always spell out what the specifics should be or how to develop the guidelines. This leaves some discretion in the hands of bureaucrats who will be crafting the exact contents of the particular policy statement, consultation paper, new law or new regulation coming out of the Minute.

9   In contrast, as a full-time advocate at Pollution Probe in 1990 and 1991, I made good strategic use of my knowledge of the government and my contacts within government.

This education process is much harder than it probably sounds for several reasons. Most bureaucrats feel disempowered by a system which requires them to spend huge amounts of time doing mundane tasks like writing letters for Ministers, briefing notes, and reports and attending meetings. It is not always stimulating work. Generally, a middle level bureaucrat in a policy-related job would directly work on only one or maybe two major cabinet submissions within a four or five year government cycle.

The other thing I noticed is that ENGOs often failed to target all the members of Cabinet. Often, strong supporters for environmental initiatives are toiling away in other Ministries and they can support innovative proposals. For example, armed with information from environmental groups working to preserve the Rouge valley, one of the senior lawyers and I helped to convince Ian Scott, the former Attorney General under Peterson Liberal government, to strongly support preserving most of the Rouge Valley in Scarborough and to pressure other cabinet members to take a new approach to Rails to Greenways development policy in the province. Unfortunately the latter initiative died when the government changed and was stalled for several years.

Obviously, the policy development process is more complex and varied than I have been able to suggest in these comments. However I don't want to spend much more time describing the policy development process today; what I really want to focus on now are the speed bumps I observed in trying to develop innovative environmental policy.

BUREAUCRATIC SPEED BUMPS

There are two types of speed bumps in the civil service I want to discuss today. First, there are those associated with certain structures of decision and policy making. These are associated with various ministries and central government ministries and agencies like the Ministry of Finance, Management Board Secretariat, Cabinet Office and the Premier's Office.

Secondly, there are speed bumps associated with the dominant paradigm about what can and cannot be discussed by policy makers. These speeds bumps are a fundamental part of the social and political ecology of the bureaucracy.

The culture of a particular Ministry involved in policy development is one of the more familiar types of structural speed bumps. As numerous commentators on public policy have observed, most ministries and agencies also have a particular culture and history this often influences how policy ideas are dealt with. I would argue that, up until very recently, the MOEE was incredibly conservative.[10] This was partly attributable to the fact that most of its original staff were drawn from the engineering fraternity, and engineers don't like new and unproven technologies and policy measures that rely on soft, nebulous notions like value and attitude change.

---

10   My first job in the Ministry of the Environment in 1980 was working as a Sewage System Inspector in the Peterborough region after I graduated from Trent with my B.Sc. in Biology. I found that, given the predominance of engineers, the culture of MOE was somewhat rowdy and vulgar.

I think that some of the structural speed bumps have been addressed to a degree by both the NDP and the Liberal governments. The Liberals launched numerous changes to the structure and function of the various central agencies and many of the line ministries in the mid 1980s and some of these were continued by the NDP when they took office in September 1990.

For example, when I joined the Policy Development Division in the Ministry of Attorney General in the summer of 1988, a massive amount of policy-making power was held by the Ministry of Treasury and Economics (which was renamed the Ministry of Finance in February 1993). Like the other key central agencies in the Ontario government at the time, Treasury had highly trained policy analysts who scrutinized every environmental cabinet submission with a magnifying glass, looking for evidence that the MOE was trying to build a new empire. Quite a few of these analysts, including Carol Harris-Lonero and Russ Houldin, were graduates of FES.

These analysts had a powerful impact on environmental policy-making and they were feared and sometimes loathed by staff in the MOEE. For example, for years Treasury staff opposed the creation of a large Blue Box system in the province because the system would be costly. In fact, if the Ontario Soft Drink Association had not come up with money to launch the program in 1985, implementation of the Blue Box system probably would have been delayed at least another three or four years.

To counter the impact of these Treasury analysts in areas of social and environmental policy and to shift more power to his Ministry, Ian Scott hired a whole bunch of bright young lawyers to beef up his policy shop in AG.

Jim Bradley, the Liberal Environment Minister from 1985 until 1990, also recognized the value of having his own stable of thoroughbred policy experts. Eventually, this group of thoroughbreds came to be known as the Fiscal Planning and Economic Analysis (FPEA) Unit of the Corporate Resources Division at MOEE. Today, the power of this unit is enormous because they are involved in drafting all MOEE Cabinet submissions, prepare most of the large briefing packages for the Minister, control many budget decisions and have access to most of the Ministry's slush funds. In effect, the FPEA Unit has become a large speed bump for policy developers in the MOEE.

I think that another type of structural speed bump has arisen out of efforts to promote better environmental planning and policy development within line ministries. Thus, many line ministries such as Economic Development and Trade, Transportation and Housing have dozens of staff working on environmental policy issues. Both the Liberal and the NDP governments also created new agencies such as the Ontario Native Affairs Secretariat, the Clean Water Agency, the Interim Waste Authority (IWA) and the Office of the Greater Toronto Area, all with significant roles in environmental planning. As a result, environmental policy development and review activities have been diffused throughout the government and policy development processes are increasingly being reformulated and reconceived to accommodate these new agencies.

Some of the new speed bumps are a consequence of social and political pressures. One of the most important of these is the *Charter of Rights and Freedoms*. As the current litigation between the MOEE and York Region over the Interim Waste Authority site search process suggests, failure to consider the use of this weapon has the potential to seriously undermine policy initiatives.

Another relatively new speed bump is the *Freedom of Information and Protection of Privacy Act*.[11] I think it is ironic that this freedom of

---

11   Amendments introduced to the *FOIPPA* by the Ontario government as part of Bill 26 on November 29, 1995 will allow heads of agencies to reduce access to documents.

information law seems to have produced in its implementation results exactly the opposite of those intended by reformers who argued for them. For example, Ontario's Act often has served to benefit corporations who can easily afford to pay the charges involved to purchase all copies of documents they want, to obtain detailed information about new technologies, other companies and government policy-making well before other stakeholders. Moreover, FOI laws have tended to discourage bureaucrats from documenting certain sensitive information that may later become subject to FOI requests. I am convinced there are lessons in this experience that should be considered as we rush toward implementation of the new *Environmental Bill of Rights*.

A related trend is the phenomenal growth of the policy community working on environmental issues. In the past decade, the environmental policy community has grown to include a huge number of environmental groups, academics, consultants, industry experts, etc. who want to be consulted about new initiatives and this makes the consultation process very long and complicated. For example, the WRO distributed more than 15,000 copies of *Regulatory Measures to Achieve Ontario's Waste Reduction Targets: Initiatives Paper No. 1* outlining the proposed 3Rs (reduction, reuse and recycling) regulations and we received thousands of pages of commentary on the proposed 3Rs regulations. We had hoped to complete the consultation process in three months but we did not finish it until nearly eighteen months later. The draft 3Rs regulations were released in late April 1993 and the final 3Rs regulations were released in March 1994, three years after the original announcement by Ruth Grier in February 1991. In many respects, this was a breakneck pace for the MOEE when this regulatory development work is compared with progress under the Municipal Industrial Strategy on Abatement (MISA) program and the Clean Air Programme, both launched by the Liberals in the late 1980s.

The increased profile of environmental issues also has increased the importance of communications and education activities and has led to a growing preoccupation with "spin doctoring" issues. While communications staff in government agencies always have played an important role in getting the message out, in the past five years spin doctors have gained more and more clout in the policy system.[12] They strongly influence the timing of policy development and what policies can be developed.

Another new speed bump is the information overload crisis. With e-mail systems and fax machines information flies around the bureaucracy very fast. This often puts pressure on staff and senior bureaucrats to come up with responses more quickly. Sometimes people will shoot from their computer keyboard hip rather than thinking for longer about what they should say and later they regret the advice they gave.

Perhaps the darkest side of the information revolution is that most senior civil servants usually never read any reports more than 100 pages long and rarely read anything longer than 50 pages. For example, my guess is that I could count on two hands the number of senior managers in the MOEE who have read even five pages from *Our Common Future* or who have read one chapter of text from the Agenda 21 document produced for the Rio Conference in June 1992.

Instead their time is consumed with fire fighting and reviewing drafts of letters, briefing notes and memos and other documents. But it means that their level of knowledge is extremely superficial. This also sets a very poor example for other staff. For example, WRO staff did not have any recent life-cycle analyses on refillable containers on hand when I arrived in July 1991. Indeed, my experience was that many MOEE bureaucrats had a "don't confuse me with the facts" attitude about the information revolution. If the reports didn't support their policy approach, they didn't want to read them or know about them.

---

12   On this point, see John O'Neill, *Ecology, Policy and Politics: Human Well-Being and the Natural World* (1993). London: Routledge.

Advisory committees are another important speed bump in
environmental policy making today.[13] I became fairly familiar with
the role of advisory committees after I was appointed to the Waste
Reduction Advisory Committee or WRAC in March 1991. Although
I attended only one meeting representing Pollution Probe, I ended up
going to about five WRAC meetings representing the WRO. Based on
my experiences, it became clear to me that many bureaucrats felt very
nervous about sharing the policy development process with these parallel
expert committees. In part, this was because members of these advisory
committees often have excellent networks and sometimes have better
information than the bureaucrats do.

Right now I would say that one of the biggest speed bumps in
the MOEE is the human resources crisis. Hiring of full-time staff is
extremely restricted and many key drivers of environmental policy-
making are on contract. About 40 percent of the WRO's staff were on
contract while I worked there and all of the staff at the Round Table were
on contract; many of us were sympathetic to what the government was
trying to do but none of us were able to secure a full time job during
the time we worked for the MOEE. And the problem is not just with
junior and middle-level staff. Both the former MOEE deputy minister,
Richard Dicerni, and Peter Victor, Assistant Deputy Minister for the
Environmental Sciences and Standards Division and a former part-time
professor here at FES, were on contract up until late 1993.[14]

---

13   The NDP government dismantled the WRAC in April 1993. The new Ontario
government sunsetted the Advisory Committee on Environmental Standards (ACES;
established in 1989) and the Environmental Assessment Advisory Committee (EAAC;
established in 1983) in late September 1995 and did not renew the mandate of the MISA
Advisory Committee established in 1987.

14   Richard Dicerni was appointed as Deputy Minister of Education and Training in
August 1995. Linda Stevens was appointed as the new Deputy at MOEE at the same
time. In the result, it could be argued that the NDP government was unable to change
the political composition of the MOEE's staff in a significant way. Thus, most bureaucrats
will continue to be small 'l' liberals or small 'c' conservatives with a smattering of a few
NDPers but not many in senior positions. And I can say that I did not meet one person
who admitted to being a member of the Green Party of Ontario.

There are some positive aspects to the proliferation of structural speed bumps in environmental policy-making. One positive response is the establishment of inter-ministerial teams to work on policy options. In addition, ministries also have begun to undertake joint consultations with other ministries because they recognize that policy issues must be dealt with in a more holistic manner.

There are several negative consequences of these structural speed bumps as well. I want to mention two of these.

a) Lack of Interest in Innovative Policy

First, I think the most important negative consequence is that innovative policy-making is seriously discouraged because people are afraid to take risks. I was told on several occasions that I was only to work on one or maybe two policy options for an important cabinet submission and that all of the others were to be set up as straw options. Research on the other options outside of what was considered acceptable often was discouraged.

In these cases, my sense was that the middle managers and assistant deputy ministers (ADMs) involved were fearful that their preferred policy options might be shelved in favour of other approaches[15]. For example, one idea I tried to push when I worked at the WRO which ended up being

---

15 As Bruce Doern and Richard Phidd point out in the second edition of their classic text, *Canadian Public Policy* (1993) there are five main policy processes in Canadian public policy.

First, there is the priority-setting process. Second, there is the expenditure process which determines how initiatives are financed. Third, there is the policy process related to taxation. Fourth, there is the regulatory process.
Fifth, there is the policy process associated with crown corporations and public enterprises.

My sense is that the last three of these processes are going to be used less and less in Ontario environmental policy making in the next decade.

partly reflected in the draft 3Rs regulations was the idea that we should give municipalities more flexibility in the design of their recycling programs. Why not, I argued, allow northern municipalities to collect more paper products to feed northern mills instead of requiring them and all other Ontario municipalities to collect heavy glass jars that probably will end up being used in road construction. However, it took staff in the Minister's office to put a modified version of this idea back into the draft 3Rs regulations because key WRO and OMMRI staff did not like my approach.

b) Environmental Policy-making on the Fly

Another phenomena I observed with increasing frequency is what some senior officials call "policy-making on the fly". The basic idea is that senior officials go into meetings with important stakeholders with a general policy approach and end up improvising specifics as required. I was told on several occasions that confidence to do this kind of policy improvisation was the mark of a good senior policy maker.

Despite, most senior policy makers believe that the public is experiencing tax fatigue and they don't feel they can sell new green taxes. We may see some modest initiatives in the 1994 budget but I would be surprised if major structural changes in the tax system are brought in at the provincial level in the next decade, despite the recommendations of the *Final Report of the Fair Tax Commission* (1993).

Traditional command and control regulation also is fading in importance. The popularity of self-assessment and voluntary compliance with regulations has expanded by leaps and bounds because of the cost of command anc control regulation.

Crown corporations have also proven to be a mixed blessing at best for the last few Ontario governments. The Ontario Waste Management Corporation is seen by many observers as a costly white elephant. Running municipal sewage treatment plants has caused many headaches for the MOEE. My guess is that the Clean Water Agency will be the last major environmental crown corporation in Ontario for quite a long time.

The need for policy-making on the fly has been influenced by the information revolution and new technologies such as e-mail and cellular phones. My concern was that this type of policy-making lacked the kind of checks and balances that is desirable in the more traditional policy development process. More importantly, I often felt that this style of policy making was incrementally undermining the decision-making authority of the Minister.

c) The Dominant Policy Paradigm

To my mind the more troubling aspect of policy making in the civil service was the dominant paradigm about what could and could not be considered a legitimate issue in developing environmental policy. For example, most bureaucrats in the MOEE have little knowledge about the international context of Canadian consumption. In other words, they are unwilling to consider the fact that Canadians consume 30 times the resources of peoples in the developing world in setting policy. Thus I often was ridiculed when I suggested that a significant reduction in first world consumption should be a legitimate policy goal.

The dominant paradigm within the bureaucracy also is remarkably anthropocentric. In the years I worked in the civil service I cannot remember words like ecology, biology and the names of wildlife species and plants rolling off the tongues of my colleagues more than a few times. All of the policy analysis we undertook had an exclusive focus on human needs and interests and I found this was very frustrating at times.

d) Lack of Understanding of Public Policy Theory

A related frustration is that many of the senior policy makers in the bureaucracy had little or no knowledge about public policy theory.

For example, Doern and Phidd describe the range of key contending approaches to Canadian public policy as including the rational, incremental pluralist, public choice, class-corporatist and comparative policy ones.

Generally, I found MOEE bureaucrats tended to invoke a mixture of rational decision theory and incremental-pluralist approaches to public policy in their analyses of policy options. At times, some even ventured into analyses based on the public choice model. However, they had little interest in the class-corporatist and comparative policy approaches. Consequently these bureaucrats often failed to capture the essence of a particular issue or policy debate. This also severely limited their horizons in conceiving options.

ECOLOGICAL TREAD MARKS

I want to speak for a few minutes about the ecological tread
marks that policy makers and decision makers have left in the Ontario
environment in the past five years.

Before I launch into my comments, I think it would be unfair not to
acknowledge that during the time I worked in government both Ontario
governments were saddled with the burden of a federal government that
was more interested in deregulation than progressive environmental
policy-making. Indeed, during the Mulroney Era, we saw cuts to VIA
Rail, the gutting of federal renewable energy policies, weak enforcement
of the *Canadian Environmental Protection Act*, the promulgation of a weak
new federal environmental assessment law, the implementation the Free
Trade Agreement and the finalization of North American Free Trade
Agreement (NAFTA).

These federal initiatives left their own ecological tread marks
and made it more difficult for the province to respond in some areas.
However, it would be unfair to blame the Mulroney government for most
of the bad provincial policies implemented in the period.

To set my comments in context, I want to return briefly to the
heady days of 1985 and 1986 when the Ontario Liberals were cranking
out major policy announcements on the environment at a breakneck
pace. This was a period in which the Municipal Industrial Strategy
on Abatement program was announced, a province-wide Blue Box

system was launched, the acid rain clampdown was begun and the prosecution rate for companies breaking environmental laws was substantially increased. Jim Bradley became something of a hero in many environmentalist circles.

But storm clouds were on the horizon, and the Ontario Liberals eventually left their share of ecological tread marks between 1988 and 1990. For example, they postponed implementation of their Clean Air Programme or CAP in the face of industry pressure. They decided to go ahead with logging in Temagami even though they knew this sent the wrong signals on First Nations self-government and sustainable development in the region. They also announced their intention to grant fast-track approvals for new landfills in the Durham and Peel regions and the Treasurer and his staff launched Project X in their efforts to speed up the approval process for development projects under the *Environmental Assessment Act*.

Unfortunately for the NDP, many of the ecological tread marks left by the Liberals have now grown over with weeds and been forgotten. However, we should not forget that the Liberals failed to undertake the kind of innovative programs that might have encouraged Ontario to become a more environment-friendly and energy efficient jurisdiction.

This meant that the NDP government faced an enormous challenge when they took office. On some fronts, they moved quickly but the results have not been great. For example, administration of the provincial Environmental Assessment process has been speeded up and, in my view, this has allowed some questionable public projects like the TTC's Spadina light-rail transit project to proceed without adequate scrutiny. In other areas, like the passage of the *Environmental Bill of Rights*, they moved more deliberately and carefully.

To their credit, the NDP have implemented many important reforms and new programs in the past three and a half years. The NDP also have passed or developed new waste management legislation, the new 3Rs regulations, new parks protection legislation and implemented numerous other legal and policy reforms. A good review of what has been done and has not been done by the current government is outlined in the December 1993 issue of the Ontario Environmental Network's Newsletter.[16]

But the NDP also have left some very wide ecological tread marks in the past three and a half years. I want to discuss three of these for the next few minutes.

a. GTA Waste Strategy

I think the most powerful example of an ecological tread mark left by the NDP government is the landfill site search process currently underway in the Greater Toronto Area or GTA.[17] Now I know what some of you are thinking – "Hey David, how can you criticize the government when they adopted the policy approach you advocated at Pollution Probe." While it is certainly true that on behalf of Pollution Probe I opposed shipping garbage to northern Ontario, and I don't think it is a sustainable option in the long term, we never said that the waste disposal site search process should be confined to agricultural land in the GTA. At Pollution Probe we opposed the Kirkland Lake option for shipping garbage north because we were worried it would destroy the source separation infrastructure for the 3Rs that we had begun to build in Ontario. We also opposed garbage incineration but this was a long-standing policy position.

The idea that the waste sites should be in the GTA was a strand of a theory that eventually became the accepted paradigm by many key advisers to the NDP government. The validity of this idea was premised

16   For an update on what the NDP accomplished, see the April 1995 edition of the OEN Newsletter.

17   The new Ontario government closed the IWA in July 1995 and cancelled the landfill site search in the GTA.

on the notion that to build serious pressure for waste reduction in Ontario, you needed to have a site search going on in the GTA.[18]

The other strands of the theory were that it was morally wrong to ship garbage to the north and that it would be illogical to ship recyclables north and then have to send them back to the GTA for use in new recycled products. One unfortunate result of the IWA landfill siting process is that a great deal of energy has been wasted on fighting these landfills and comparatively little has gone into promoting the 3Rs in the GTA.

---

18 Bill Twatio, The stuff of dreams in Kirkland Lake, Toronto Star – January 16, 1998. In the spring of 1990, the Adams iron ore mine closed, putting 325 out of work.

Twatio observes: "Metro Toronto politicians, faced with a world-class garbage problem, were soon casting, covetous glances northward at the gigantic open pits.

A marriage of convenience was arranged, with Metro spending $2.4 million on an option to buy the mine site. The town, in turn, held a referendum with 69 per cent voting in favour of conducting a study into the feasibility of using the pits as a dump. Under the terms of the agreement, 1.5 million tones of garbage a year would be shipped directly to the site on the Ontario Northland Railway, which would recoup revenue lost due to the closure of the mine. Kirkland Lake would receive an estimated $50 million over 20 years n tonnage fees, $600,000 a year in lieu of taxes, free garbage disposal worth $10 million, 150 full-time jobs, and a recycling plant worth $40 million.

Local wags were quick to revise the town slogan, with predictable result. Others, for the first time, were heard to speak favourably of Toronto. A few were known to cheer for the Leafs.

The newly elected NDP government immediately scuttled the agreement. Environment Minister Ruth Grier, obsessed with the idea that waste must be disposed of where it is produced, set up a $17.4 million Greater Toronto Interim Waste Authority to scour regional backyards for likely sites. In June, 1992, the authority identified 57 potential sites in York, Durham, and Peel regions, infuriating environmentalists and politicians.

Metro Chairman Alan Tonks fumed that the "rail haul to Kirkland Lake is going to look awfully good by the time the public is done with this government." At Winter Carnival in Kirkland Lake, the centerpiece was an 8-metre high ice sculpture of Ruth Grier, dubbed "Ruthless," depicting the minister riding a broom [and obviously intended to be portrayed as a witch]."

Moreover, during this period the Ministry turned a blind eye to export of solid waste to the USA and also allowed a considerable amount of illegal dumping of solid waste and biomedical wastes on First Nations lands. This has seriously undermined the credibility of the MOEE on their garbage export ban.

To my mind, one of the tragic aspects about the waste policy decisions the new government made is that a person I enormously respect and admire, Ruth Grier, was boxed into a corner on the issue. She ended up blowing all of her political capital on this one issue and has lost influence with her colleagues. I just hope that history will be kinder to her than the Toronto press has been.

b. Beer Can Tax

The second example of an ecological tread mark left by the current government is the beer can tax that was developed by the Ministry of Consumer and Commercial Relations and announced in the April 1992 budget. This tax boosted the price for domestic beer in cans by about $2.40 per case of 24 cans. But the measure was really intended to increase the relative price of American beer which is sold almost exclusively in cans and could have begun to glut the Ontario market beginning in the spring of 1992 if the government had not acted.

I personally support this policy; in it we see a convergence between positive protectionism or fair trade and environmental goals. By imposing the tax the Ontario government has temporarily postponed an inevitable assault on Ontario's beer industry and the thousands of workers who make beer and run the Brewer's Retail network.

Unfortunately, this measure also had the potential to affect Ontario workers who were canning domestic beer and there was no labour adjustment program for the affected workers; indeed the Ministry of

Labour and the Ministry of Industry, Trade and Technology (as it then was) were not even seriously consulted on this policy. While few workers were directly affected by the measure, at a minimum retraining programs should have been put in place to assist them. Moreover, it was hard to defend this policy because the MOEE refused to agree to allow a tax on other non-refillable soft drink and juice containers even though the environmental performance of these containers was ten times worse than that of beer cans.

The ecological tread marks left on Queen's Park by this revamped tax are difficult to assess. Among other things the furor over the beer can tax helped to convince staff in the then Ministry of Treasury and Economics that green taxes weren't such a great idea after all.

c. Scrap Tire Recycling

The current policy on scrap tire recycling is my third and last example of an ecological tread mark. Essentially the government has decided that, in the post-Hagersville Tire Fire era, tires in Ontario are to be recycled rather than burned in cement kilns or other incineration facilities.

I did not work directly on this issue at the WRO but I did become familiar with much of the literature and I am convinced that within two years or even less a study will be published showing that the current Ontario tire policy is a large net contributor to global warming. To implement this policy, millions of kilowatt hours of electricity are being used in Ontario each year to shred tires and then reprocess the shredded rubber into products with markets that are doubtful at best. But even if the markets were great I now see that it is a bad idea to use millions of kilowatts of electricity, some of which is produced by burning dirty coal, to shred tires and then recycle the by-products to produce marginal products. Instead, I now believe that most scrap tires should be burned to generate cleaner electricity or provide a substitute heat energy for imported oil and, in my last few months at the WRO, I tried to push this approach.

In addition, I believe much more emphasis should be placed on waste reduction by educating drivers to maintain their tires properly (*ie.* properly inflated tires last much longer) and on encouraging manufacturers to produce longer-lasting tires.

CONCLUSIONS

To sum up, I think that the widths are narrower and the depths are shallower than the tracks left by previous governments, but the tread marks left by the NDP government on the Ontario environment will be evident for generations.

It seems to me that many of the NDP policy initiatives were problematic because they failed to consider relevant options that might have improved decision making.

On a personal note, my experiences in the civil service have been very challenging and enjoyable. I have been fortunate in working under three administrations with different styles and visions. I also have been lucky to work on environmental policy-making from numerous angles. I think they made me a better and humbler person and I have become more modest in my expectations of fellow civil servants. But I guess most people would become more humble after they crashed a few times doing wheelies off bureaucratic speed bumps and left a least a few major ecological tread marks.

Biographical Note on the Author

When this paper was originally presented, David McRobert was Senior Policy and Research Analyst at the Workplace Health and Safety

Agency in Toronto. Between 1994 and 2010, he was In-House Counsel and Senior Policy Analyst at the Environmental Commissioner of Ontario.

David holds a B.Sc. in Biology from Trent University (1980), a Masters in Environmental Studies (M.E.S.) from York University (1984), and LL.B. from Osgoode Hall Law School (1987). Between July 1991 and May 1993 David was a senior policy advisor working on several policy and regulatory projects related to 3Rs activities for the Waste Reduction Office in the Ontario Ministry of the Environment. He was one of several WRO staff involved with public hearings on the *Waste Management Act, 1992,* one of the most controversial environmental laws in Ontario history.

Before joining the Waste Reduction Office, David coordinated research on waste management and global warming at Pollution Probe in Toronto, Ontario in 1990 and 1991. In the late 1980s, he worked for the Ministry of Attorney General and the Ministry of Labour in the Ontario government. He also worked as Community Liaison Coordinator at the Ontario Round Table on Environment and Economy for most of 1993. He was fortunate to article in the Ministry of Attorney General in 1988-89 and was heavily influenced by Steve Fram, one the innovative leaders in developing consensus processes for reforming laws in Ontario and Canada.

David has published numerous articles and reports on environmental issues in the past twenty-five years.

www.ingramcontent.com/pod-product-compliance
Lightning Source LLC
Chambersburg PA
CBHW031335290526
45784CB00014B/2759